A SIMPLE GUIDE TO BIBLE STUDY

A SIMPLE GUIDE TO BIBLE STUDY

Jack Hay

John Ritchie Publishing

40 Beansburn, Kilmarnock, Scotland

ISBN-13: 978 1 912522 97 2

www.ritchiechristianmedia.co.uk

Typeset by John Ritchie Ltd., Kilmarnock
Printed by Bell & Bain Ltd., Glasgow

Contents

Chapter 1

THE VALUE OF THE SCRIPTURES

Before embarking on some simple advice about Bible study, it is important to establish just how central the Scriptures are in a believer's life. Prior to conversion, we were in the dark about salvation, but the Scriptures made us "wise unto salvation through faith which is in Christ Jesus" (2 Tim 3.15). Either by reading the Bible for ourselves, or having its truths explained through personal witnessing or public preaching, a shaft of Gospel light penetrated the darkness of our blinded minds. Until then, we were in unbelief, but hearing the Word of God dispelled that unbelief; "faith cometh by hearing, and hearing by the word of God" (Rom 10.17). We were unregenerate, but the Word of God was crucial in effecting the new birth; "born again … by the word of God, which liveth and abideth for ever" (1 Pet 1.23). That same Word of God which was such a major factor in our conversion now plays a vital role in our development as believers; it is "**profitable** for doctrine, for reproof, for correction, for instruction in righteousness" (2 Tim 3.16).

Growth

To get the flow of thought in Peter's first epistle, ignore the division between the first two chapters. As quoted above, the Word of God was instrumental in effecting the new birth (1 Pet 1.23). Peter goes on to show that that same Word of God is necessary for spiritual growth. "As newborn babes, desire the sincere milk of the word, that ye may grow thereby" (1 Pet 2.2). Some passages of Scripture teach that to be baby-like is to our shame, but Peter makes the point that in one sense we really should be like babies. Our craving for the Word of God should be comparable to a baby's insatiable appetite for the mother's milk.

In the physical realm, a miserable appetite results in stunted growth and bodily weakness; there is a parallel in the spiritual realm. Spiritual growth and strength are dependant among other things on having a hunger for the Word of God. That is why it is so important to read it consistently, treating it as you would your regular meals; you need to approach it systematically, and in a disciplined way. To extend the analogy, the growth of a child is not perceptible with every passing meal. It is with hindsight and the passing of time that we see the progress that has been achieved. Similarly, every session with your Bible will not disclose noticeable spiritual growth, but when you stand still, and look back to where you have come from, the cumulative effect of these times with the Scriptures will become evident. I emphasise that in case you become discouraged by just how slow your advance in Bible knowledge and spiritual growth appear to be. Get this first point then - **reading the Bible is necessary for growth.**

Guidance

There are many hazards along the road of life. The prevailing immoral conditions and the very low standards of integrity can exert a negative influence. Also, the wide range of pleasures available in the world can become attractive to us. Added to that, the drive to clutter our lives with bigger and better things can induce spiritual inertia. How can a believer navigate a course through this minefield? Where can he find guidance about the legitimacy of life choices? Is there direction for even the less significant decisions that he faces? The main source of guidance is the Word of God. "Thy word is a lamp unto my feet, and a light unto my path" (Ps 119.105).

The direct commands of the Word and its overarching principles provide the seeking soul with a road-map for life, steering him away from the threats to his spiritual well-being, and channelling him into options that will count for eternity. "The entrance of thy words giveth light" (Ps 119.130). So, **reading the Bible is necessary for guidance**.

Godliness

Godliness is a reverence for God that results in holy living and devoted service, and the Scriptures play an important role in promoting this respectful attitude of heart. Acknowledging "the truth" of God's revelation is linked with godliness (Tit 1.1). It follows then that those who really want to "live soberly, righteously, and godly in this present world" (Tit 2.12) are people who will make a lot of time for pondering the Word of God. "Thy word have I hid in mine heart, that I might not sin against thee" (Ps 119.11). We were told when we were young, "Either this Book will keep you from sin, or sin will keep you from this Book". (A handwritten note on the flyleaf of John Bunyan's Bible).

Not only does the Word of God keep us from sinning, but it also has a cleansing effect upon our lives. Initially we were cleansed from our sins at conversion because of the precious shed blood of the Lord Jesus (Rev 1.5), but it has to be acknowledged that we live in a defiling world where there is so much that taints our thinking, and if permitted, would lead to bad behaviour. How can these influences be resisted? How can their effects be minimized? That question was posed and answered by the writer of Psalm 119. "Wherewithal shall a young man cleanse his way? By taking heed thereto according to thy word" (v.9). A pathway of holy conduct is dependent on reading and obeying the Word of God. The Lord Jesus said, "Ye are clean through the word that I have spoken unto you" (Jn 15.3).

This is pictured in the ancient tabernacle in the wilderness. A laver was positioned between the door of the tabernacle and the brazen altar. Priests who had been ceremonially washed all over at their initial consecration had to continually wash their hands and feet at the laver (Ex 40.7,12,30-32). It illustrates that the initial cleansing we experienced at conversion has to be followed by the constant cleansing that the laver of the Word of God provides. **Reading the Bible is necessary for godliness**.

We have established that Scripture reading is necessary for growth, for guidance and for godliness. I suggest then that you adopt a reading plan. Some are available that ensure that you get through the whole Bible in a year and that can be helpful. But even without a ready-made plan, organise your reading so that there is variety. For example, you might want to have two Old Testament sections and one New Testament section being covered in a day. Just to start at Genesis and work your way through will lead you to toiling with difficult sections day after day. (All Scripture is profitable, but it is true to say that some parts are more difficult than others)! So vary your reading; advice that I was given was, never be too long away from the Gospels!

When Moses was speaking about the beauties of the promised land, he described it as "A land of wheat, and barley, and vines, and fig trees, and pomegranates; a land of oil olive, and honey; a land wherein thou shalt eat bread without scarceness, thou shalt not lack anything in it" (Deut 8.8-9). All of the crops and fruits mentioned were on the surface of the ground, to be taken and enjoyed, and every one of them would contribute to a balanced diet to maintain the health of the people. So, right on the surface of the Word of God, there are truths to be enjoyed and appropriated, all contributing to our spiritual health. But then Moses added this; "a land whose stones are iron, and out of whose hills thou mayest dig brass (v.8b). The purpose of this booklet is to encourage "digging" into the rich veins of ore that lie beneath the surface, thoughts and truths that can be unearthed by diligent Bible study.

Chapter 2

THE STRUCTURE OF THE SCRIPTURES

When reading the Bible for the first time, many are like an Ethiopian man who had difficulty in understanding (Acts 8.30-31). It is a complex volume incorporating a library of 66 different books. It includes history and prophecy, ethics and morals, and facts about God and man.

Structure

There are two major sections, the Old and New Testaments. Everything in the Old Testament took place before the incarnation of Christ whereas the New Testament begins with His birth, and moves on from there. For the more part, the Old Testament was written in Hebrew, and the New Testament was written in Greek.

The Old Testament has three main sections. The Lord Jesus indicated these when He spoke to His disciples on the resurrection evening. He spoke about the law of Moses, the prophets and the psalms (Lk 24.44). So the three divisions are as follows;

1.	**Genesis to Esther**	**History**
2.	**Job to Song of Solomon**	**Poetry**
3.	**Isaiah to Malachi**	**Prophecy**

Each section holds valuable lessons for Christians so do not neglect the Old Testament, for "whatsoever things were written aforetime were written for our learning" (Rom 15.4).

The New Testament has three main parts. In the upper room, the Lord Jesus suggested these three sections when speaking of the work of the Holy Spirit. He said that the Spirit would "guide you into all truth" (Jn 16.13). That would be the doctrinal area of the New Testament. "He will shew you things to come" (v.13), the Book of Revelation. "He shall receive of mine, and shall shew it unto you" (v.14), the four Gospels. The three divisions are as follows then;

1. **Matthew to John**…The Gospels - records of the life, death and resurrection of the Lord Jesus Christ.

2. **The Acts of the Apostles to Jude** - the story of the spread of the Gospel, and the development of the early church, followed by the epistles which contain Christian doctrine, and outline standards of Christian behaviour.

3. **Revelation**. Mainly, future events.

Authorship

From a human standpoint, almost forty men were used to write the Bible. This was over a period of around 1600 years in places as far apart as Babylon in the east and Rome in the west. Despite differences of background and location, their messages dovetail. When critics speak of contradictions in the Bible, invariably they are lifting statements from their context. The consistency of the Bible's message is one of the evidences that **the Bible is inspired by God; He is the Author** (2 Tim 3.16). It is not the product of human brilliance, but a revelation from God. The manner of inspiration is explained by Peter when he says that "holy men of God spake as they were moved by the Holy Ghost" (2 Pet 1.21). (The word 'moved' carries the thought of a sailing ship being moved along by the wind). On occasions, the men who wrote had no clear understanding of what they were writing (1 Pet 1.10-12), a proof that their thoughts were not their own.

The Bible's critics claim that it is at variance with science. **It is at variance with scientific theories, but not with scientific facts.** For example, at a time when it was generally accepted that the world was flat, the Bible spoke of "the circle of the earth"! (Is 40.22).

Proof of its divine inspiration is seen in the fulfilment of its prophecies, particularly its predictions about the Lord Jesus. His birthplace was prophesied, as were the circumstances of His death - the betrayal, the scourging, the gambling for His clothes and the crucifixion. The Bible was inspired right to the letter, every "jot and tittle"; a 'jot' is a Hebrew letter and a 'tittle' just part of a Hebrew letter, possibly the equivalent of the stroke of a 't' or the dot of an 'i' in our alphabet (Mt 5.18). Not only were its concepts inspired by God but the very words that were employed to clothe and communicate these truths, "**words**...which the Holy Ghost teacheth" (1 Cor 2.13). The writers were given no latitude in their choice of language.

Subject

The central theme of the Bible is the Lord Jesus Christ Himself; "the scriptures...they are they which testify of me" (Jn 5.39); "in all the scriptures the things concerning himself" (Lk 24.27). In particular, His death occupies a prominent place in the Word, and in the following lines when I use the term "the cross" it stands for all that transpired there, the Person involved, the sacrifice that was made, the work that was accomplished. There are; **The Figures of the Cross** in the books of Moses, for example, the Passover lamb (Ex 12). **The Foreshadowings of the Cross** in the prophets, such as in Isaiah ch.53.

The Feelings of the Cross are laid bare in psalms like Psalms 22 and 69.

The Facts of the Cross are documented in the four Gospels, the harsh vicious record of human brutality.

The Fruits of the Cross are outlined in the Acts and the Epistles, the endless flow of spiritual blessings enjoyed by those who believe.

The Freshness of the Cross is stressed in the book of Revelation, as the Lord Jesus is depicted as "a Lamb as it had been slain" (Rev 5.6). This volume is intended to encourage Bible study, but whether reading or studying more carefully, always be on the lookout for your Saviour, and doubtless you will find precious nuggets of truth that will warm your heart.

Chapter 3

ATTITUDE TO BIBLE STUDY

Meditation

We now consider what should be an appropriate attitude towards the Word of God. In our first chapter, the stress was on the fact that every believer should read the Scriptures in a consistent diligent way to facilitate spiritual growth. However, there is an advance on simply reading, and that is to give serious thought to what is being read. The old fashioned word that the Bible uses to describe that is "meditate". A blessing is pronounced on people whose "delight is in the law of the Lord; and in his law doth he **meditate** day and night" (Ps 1.1-2). It would take us off-track to explore the many references in the psalms to meditation - how we should meditate, what we should meditate, and on whom we should meditate. That might be a profitable early study for you as you begin to take the Bible seriously!

A major Old Testament character and a notable New Testament

character were both instructed to meditate on the Word of God. When Joshua succeeded Moses, among the instructions he was given was this; "This book of the law shall not depart out of thy mouth; but thou shalt **meditate** therein day and night, that thou mayest observe to do according to all that is written therein: for then thou shalt make thy way prosperous, and then thou shalt have good success" (Josh 1.8). Meditation on the Word of God, and subsequent obedience to the Word of God would be crucial factors in ensuring his success. Things have never changed. Key elements contributing to a happy and fruitful Christian life are a willingness to think in-depth as you read the Bible, and to submissively comply with the instructions it contains.

Timothy was the New Testament character who was encouraged to meditate. "**Meditate** upon these things; give thyself wholly to them; that thy profiting (progress) may appear to all" (1 Tim 4.15). Very few other translations use the word "meditate" in the verse, but that concept is embedded in the Greek word, along with the idea of diligence and care. Paul had listed some of Timothy's duties, including the public reading of the Word with exhortations and teaching. So he was being encouraged to firmly set his mind not only on his responsibilities, but also on the content of what he was reading and teaching. If he did, it would be evident to all that he was making spiritual progress. Once more, the lesson is that meditation on the things of God is essential for spiritual growth. Hurried surface reading will not have the same impact. A rushed race through a couple of chapters just for the satisfaction of seeing them ticked off as having been "done" will not yield the same benefits as a thoughtful perusal of the passage.

Memorising

There is value in memorising Scripture, and even in Sunday Schools we encourage the young people to learn verses and passages by heart. However, it has to be acknowledged that not everyone has the same capacity for memorisation. You may discover though, that if you diligently study the Scriptures, without realising it, your constant occupation with the verses gets them firmly etched on your memory. I could not do this now because age definitely affects the memory, but many years ago, with a little prompting here and there, I could recite the whole of 1 Peter. It wasn't that I had made a conscious effort to memorise it: the fact that my mind was being constantly exposed to it as I studied it got it firmly into my brain.

If you do have a clear mind, memorising the Word can be helpful. Quite some years ago, I was given a brand new Newberry Bible just when I was embarking on a week of Bible teaching on the Epistle to the Ephesians. I offered the Bible to any young person who could recite the first chapter of the epistle. It cost me dearly! Quite a few made the attempt and I had to buy a few more copies to keep my side of the bargain. I was happy about that though. Two sisters who served the Lord in Zambia, Miss Rowntree and Miss Warke, used to tell of a boy in their Sunday School who won a pair of boots for reciting the whole of the Gospel by Mark!

Diligent Study

"Study to show thyself approved unto God, a workman that needeth not to be ashamed, rightly dividing the word of truth"

(2 Tim 2.15 AV). "Do your best to present yourself to God as one approved, a worker who has no need to be ashamed, rightly handling the word of truth" (ESV). "Strive diligently to present thyself approved to God, a workman that has not to be ashamed, cutting in a straight line the word of truth" (JND). "Do your best to present yourself to God as one approved, a workman who does not need to be ashamed and who correctly handles the word of truth" (NIV). I have deliberately quoted various translations of 2 Timothy 2.15, for it is a verse that is fundamental to the thrust of this booklet. (The abbreviations for the translations will be explained later). You will note that the word "study" is used by what used to be called the Authorised Version (AV), now more commonly referred to as the King James Version (KJV). The word does not refer to Bible study, but rather to the diligence that should mark us as we are ambitious to gain God's approval. However, our ability to handle God's Word aright contributes to that approval, "rightly dividing the word of truth".

This verse also infers that to be deficient in this could bring shame. Just to have some vague idea of the contents of the Bible will never bring divine approval. So while the word "study" in our verse does not refer to Bible study, it is clear that earnest Bible study will contribute to us being approved by God, when we are able to rightly handle the word of truth. Acquiring an accurate knowledge of God's Word and learning to apply it in the right way does not come overnight. There is no such thing as a crash course in Bible study; it is naïve to think that. It takes painstaking application and time-consuming study; this is why Paul uses the word "workman". If you tend to have a lazy mind and a very limited concentration span, you would need to be willing to make the effort to change. You would have to ask God to help you to focus your thoughts, and give you the determination to get down to some hard work. The Bereans "**searched** the scriptures daily" (Acts 17.11). To discover the truths of Scripture demanded a search, and it was a persistent search, for they did it "daily". A superficial hurried scanning of the Word would never have unearthed treasures of truth for them to enjoy. They had to dig deeper; are you prepared for that?

So I have called this chapter "attitude". Before you start getting real as far as Bible study is concerned, you will have to prepare yourself to be a workman or woman, focused, earnest, undistracted, persistent even when you become discouraged at the difficulties or the seeming lack of progress. Perhaps some preachers have given you the impression that every moment with your Bible will bring feelings of elation and joy. That is unrealistic; I repeat, **Bible Study involves hard work**. Those of you who are involved with studies for school or further education know that you have to apply your mind to the task of learning; it is the same with Bible study. Paul said to Timothy, "**Consider what I say**; and the Lord give thee understanding in all things" (2 Tim 2.7). The Lord will not give you the understanding of what you read if you are unwilling to give it serious consideration. Getting your mind-set right is of the utmost importance. Approach the task with the prayer of the psalmist on your lips; "Open thou mine eyes, that I may behold wondrous things out of thy law" (Ps 119.18).

Chapter 4

THE CLOCK AND THE CLOSET

The Importance of a Schedule

Whatever stage you are at in life, there will be huge demands on your time. Many of these demands are legitimate. If you have embarked on an academic course, your studies should be addressed responsibly and seriously. In learning a trade, you may have courses to attend in addition to the hours on the job. Generally, people in employment are committed to their employers for around 40 hours each week. Bringing up a family demands apportioning time to the needs of the children; and so life is busy, and there never seems to be an excess of time.

In addition to these demands, regular assembly meetings can occupy around ten hours a week including travel time. There will be other Bible teaching opportunities you will want to take advantage of, using up more of your available time. Local assembly commitments are not optional, but mandatory obligations for every assembly member; "not forsaking the assembling of ourselves together, as the manner of some is" is a command (Heb 10.25). Never be tempted to miss a meeting for the sake of personal Bible study.

So, for most people life does seem to be hectic, a frenzied rush from one activity to the next. How can a schedule for Bible study fit in to these wide-ranging demands on our time? Very simply, by **making the time** for it. Generally we can find time for the things that we really want to do. The keep-fit enthusiast finds time for the gym. The budding artist finds time for the art class. The lad who enjoys kicking a ball around will book a pitch for an evening with his friends. The golf course can easily take four hours of valuable time. Social media can become addictive, and swallow up endless hours. It is possible that in order to make time for Bible study, other things will have to be sacrificed. It is a case of prioritising activities to ensure that the things that matter most are not neglected. Make sure that whatever the pressures, you factor in time for Bible study.

There could even be a danger of spending so much time in Christian service, as we plan for it and engage in it, that we ignore the thing that will make it more effective, the diligent study of the Word of God. Martha was doing a very noble thing in serving the Lord Jesus, but she let it get on top of her, and she allowed the lack of co-operation on Mary's part to annoy her. By contrast, Mary "sat at Jesus feet, and heard his word" (Lk 10.39), and the Lord indicated that Mary had "chosen that good part" (v.42). You have the ability to choose what you do with your time, and you could elect to devote a suitable amount of time to what could be seen as the equivalent of sitting at His feet, the earnest study of the Holy Scriptures. When the Lord Jesus called His disciples, He had two specific targets for them, first that "they should be with him", and then, "that he might send them forth to preach" (Mk 3.14). Note the balance; spending time with Him would energise them for going out to preach. Update the concept; spending time with His Word will equip you for the service to which He has called you.

The Need for Solitude

There are few who opt for a hermit life-style. Most of us are to some extent social beings, and the company of kindred spirits is one of the joys of life. However, there are circumstances where solitude is necessary. One of these situations is for the pursuit of personal Bible study. There were spells in the lives of some Bible heroes when they were out of the limelight, spending time with God. Moses was in Midian for forty years (Ex 2). Elijah was told, "hide thyself" (1 Kgs 17.3). John the Baptist was "in the deserts till the day of his shewing unto Israel" (Lk 1.80). Paul "went into Arabia" (Gal 1.17). Away from the public eye, and in touch with God, they absorbed His truth, and formed convictions that strengthened character and invigorated them for days of service. These were times of spiritual education in isolation with God.

In citing these examples I am only highlighting the principle that at times it is necessary to step back from activities others are involved in to spend time alone with God in Bible study. I am not suggesting that you drop out of college or take a year out for intensive Bible study. All I am saying is that there will be occasions when you will have to be alone with Him, away from the crowd. It is what the Lord Jesus called entering into your closet and shutting the door (Mt 6.6). This may mean foregoing the companionship of friends, even when they have exciting plans for the day! Those friends may even criticise you. They may accuse you of being anti-social or of feeling super spiritual. They would understand it if you are "studying for a meeting", but preparation for preaching is not the main reason for studying the Scriptures. Never allow yourself to be forced into being involved with something secondary if you have determined to set aside a certain period of time to be alone with God.

It is not only people who can intrude into our quiet times and cause distractions. The beeps and buzzes of a mobile phone or other gadgets can disturb our concentration If you are the kind of person who is easily distracted and who finds it difficult to refocus, perhaps the best course of action would be to banish the offending article to another room, or have it switched off altogether.

Chapter 5

POSTURE, PAPER AND PEN

A Desk

When it comes to Bible study, there are some practical things that are helpful, and they are available to us. Believers of a past generation were less favoured as far as a good study environment was concerned. Many of them lived in overcrowded homes, and the cramped conditions made it difficult to get the peace and quiet that is necessary for diligent learning. However, they were not deterred, and their knowledge of the Bible could put our generation to shame. An acquaintance of mine was brought up as one of a large family in a mining community. The only place in the house where he could be alone to study was in a large unlit cupboard under the stair. He read and studied wearing a miner's helmet with its lamp!

Most parents these days provide a desk as part of the bedroom furniture, and it is preferable to use a desk while studying. An easy chair does not lend itself to earnest study; there is the danger of becoming too comfortable or even sleepy! Elisha had a bed to sleep in, but for study there was "a table, and a stool, and a candlestick" (2 Kgs 4.10). So if available, a desk and chair are helpful for Bible study.

Pen and Paper

I am a child of the pre-computer age, so for Bible study I was dependent on what John calls "paper and ink" (2 Jn 12), or "ink and pen" (3 Jn 13). So for what it is worth, I will explain how I went about it with these primitive tools! I always used margined paper, writing the Bible book and chapter number on the top line. Then in the margin I would put the verse number, and against it jotted down what I had noted from the verse. This might be a paraphrase of the verse in my own words. The meaning of some of the words as they were in the original language would be noted as explained in a concordance or Bible dictionary. Possibly an illustration of the teaching of the verse from some Bible story from the history of either the Old or New Testaments would be incorporated. There might be references to other passages where similar thoughts are expressed. You may want to leave a line or two between verses so that you can make additional notes when you come back to it on a future occasion.

You will see that I have never relied on memory. This is a very important point, for even the best of memories cannot retain every thought, every thrilling discovery, and every treasure that the Scriptures hold. There was an occasion when a middle-aged brother saw me studying the Bible with pen in hand. He told me that a great regret of his life was the fact that although he had read the Bible extensively, it took him fourteen years to start noting his findings. He had been relying on a good memory and now it was letting him down!

Should you decide to follow the pattern that I found helpful, avoid making your notes on scraps of paper that can easily be mislaid. Use a proper notebook, or a pad with pages that can be filed in a ring binder or something similar. Make sure that the time and effort put into your meticulous study is not wasted by you losing the fruit of your labours. Ensure that you have a permanent record.

For many of you, the foregoing may seem very old fashioned. From your earliest you have been accustomed to a keyboard, and there is no doubt that your laptop could prove to be a valuable asset when getting down to study. What I have outlined above can easily be adapted to suit your normal way of noting things on your computer. You have the added advantage of being able to make additions without difficulty, and of even revising your view about the meaning of some phrase by means of the delete button. You can add new thoughts as they come to you, or as you hear them suggested by others. As in the previous paragraph, a word of caution; make sure that you keep saving your work and that you have adequate back-up. It would be a shame if hours of hard work were to be wasted. A file could be created for every Bible book and every theme that you study.

Some of the points from my own experience outlined in these paragraphs were matters on which I received valuable information from an older man in our district. He was a meticulous Bible student himself, and was very happy to suggest tips that would assist younger people who were showing some interest in studying the Scriptures. It may be that there is someone in your area who could be of considerable help in sharing with you details of their study methods. Obviously, there is no fixed pattern, for everyone has their own style, but try to benefit from all the advice that you can get in this important area of your life. Don't be slow to approach anyone whom you feel could be of help; they will be delighted to assist you all they can.

Some friends of mine were very meticulous in their records; they had a manilla folder for every book of the Bible. Whenever valuable thoughts came to them either in their personal reading or at meetings, these were documented and filed in the appropriate place. I mention this for the benefit of those who would have the patience to follow their example. In that generation, they needed a filing cabinet; your computer will do the job if you just take a few minutes to type up any notes that you have made in a meeting!

Chapter 6

GETTING STARTED

Budgeting

From time to time your Bible study will involve you in some expense although hints around birthday and Christmas time may slash the cost! People who have hobbies are willing for the expenditure that the hobby entails, and often people devote fairly substantial amounts of their income to what they regard as the pleasures of their leisure time. I am not suggesting that Bible study ranks with hobbies and entertainments, but I am simply making the point that if unsaved people are willing to spend lavishly on what they enjoy, it would seem strange if the people of God were reluctant to devote some of their resources to something as vital to their Christian lives as Bible study.

Getting started then will involve a little bit of an outlay, but you can add further study aids as and when finances allow. There are a number of basic requirements that will have to be purchased, and if the budget is limited, it is worthwhile looking around for second-hand bargains.

Bibles

Even with what is regarded as its old fashioned language, the Bible translation that is known as the Authorised Version (AV) or the King James Version (KJV), is still a basic English requirement for Bible study. It is based on what is called the *Textus Receptus*, a Latin term meaning, the Received Text. To a large extent, subsequent translations claim to be based on manuscripts that are deemed to be more recently discovered, but dating to earlier centuries. Not everyone accepts the validity of these earlier manuscripts. I was brought up in an environment where the Revised Version (RV) of 1885 was often referred to, or the New Translation by John Nelson Darby (NT or JND) of 1890. Possibly that is why I still refer to these versions, although I make the Authorised Version the basis for my personal reading and study, and the version from which I consistently read in a public meeting.

The New King James Version (NKJV) updates the Elizabethan language of the old version without deviating from the Received Text. Other modern translations such as The New International Version (NIV) and the English Standard Version (ESV) are based on other manuscripts. Making reference to a modern version can sometimes elucidate an archaic word or phrase, but it is helpful to make the AV the basis for study, not only from the point of view of its accuracy and dignity, but also because so many Bible word study books are based upon it.

Very few people are completely satisfied with any translation, and it would be easy to find the translation of a verse here or there in each of them that we feel to be inferior to other renderings, or maybe even misleading. That said, we should exercise caution, and it would be wise to exclude from our bookshelves versions that appear to have a doctrinal agenda that is at odds with what we know to be the truth of God. Some are decidedly casual, almost irreverent, and unworthy of being taken seriously by the Bible student. Be aware too that some of these so called "translations" are really paraphrases that make no attempt to accurately convey the sense of the original text. This is not an endorsement, but the modern translation that seems to me to retain more dignity than others is the ESV. The way it treats the first few verses of 1 Corinthians 11 is disappointing, but as was stated earlier, most of us find flaws in any translation we examine.

Many Bible teachers use what we generally call the Newberry Bible. (I keep it handy for reference). The Newberry Bible is available in different formats, but one of its main advantages is a system of symbols that indicates the precise tense of every verb. Like everything else, it will take time and effort to get to grips with it, but then with usage, it will become familiar and easy. It has often been said that in understanding a verse, we need to know the tense to get the sense! To those who have no knowledge of Hebrew or Greek, the Newberry Bible is valuable in explaining the verb tense, or the precise meaning of a preposition, or a word that is emphasised in the original language.

Another valuable help is a Bible with a good central margin.

Its a-z references against words in the text will link you to the margin where parallel passages will be highlighted. In this way you can compare what you are reading with similar teaching elsewhere in Scripture. For example, a reference to servants in Ephesians 6.5 may link you up with what Peter has to say to servants in 1 Peter 2.18.

Books

Until recent years, a concordance was a big heavy book that people placed on anything that had to be flattened out! With the digital age, the need for such a massive volume has gone. However, a paragraph on the use of concordances might be helpful. The one that most people used was *Strong's Concordance*. One of its purposes was to assist in finding a verse you knew, but could not remember where it was in Scripture. For example, you could be thinking about the Lord Jesus as the shepherd as you read John 10. It comes to your mind that elsewhere He is called the "great shepherd of the sheep", but where is that phrase found? Looking up the word "shepherd", and finding a list of every occurrence of that word, you will find that your verse is Hebrews 13.20.

In addition to helping you to locate verses, the concordance also gives details of the different shades of meaning connected with a particular word. A number appears against each reference, and checking the number at the back of the concordance reveals the different ways that the word is translated throughout Scripture.

All the benefits of a concordance are now available in digital form on your phone or computer. Using the Online Bible or e-Sword for example, simply bring up your passage, enable Strong's, and a number will appear against every word. Click on the number beside the word that you want to investigate, and all the data will be there. Should you require a list of every usage of the word in Scripture, click on the search icon, enter the number, and the list will appear. You may get some surprises; for example, in 1 John 2.24, the Greek word *meno* (number G3306) is translated by three different English words, "abide", "remain" and "continue"! Discoveries like this will make your Bible study interesting, even exciting.

Vine's Expository Dictionary, is another helpful word study book, particularly the New Testament section which is far more extensive than the Old Testament volume. Mr Vine's wide knowledge of the Greek language provides invaluable insights into the various shades of meaning connected with Greek words. Word studies are interesting, but do not become so bogged down with studying individual words that you lose the meaning and beauty of the passage. We might describe that as failing to see the wood for the trees!

Chapter 7

WHERE TO START

Choosing a Book

It would be important to pray about where to start studying, but some guidance could be forthcoming from a number of directions. It could be that in your recent daily readings a certain Bible book has caught your interest. Maybe the schedule for study at the assembly mid-week meeting could provide you with an idea of which book to start with. It is important that everyone should go to these meetings prepared, and if you are a young man, you might be keen to start making little contributions to the discussions. Another factor could be that hearing the exposition of a passage has given you an appetite for that particular book.

Having decided where to start, before getting down to your studies, read and re-read the book in question. Do so with pen in hand, and look out for certain things. See if there are any recurring themes, or words that are repeated. As you read, avoid stopping automatically at the end of the chapter. A man called Stephen Langton is credited with dividing the Scriptures into chapters and verses back in the 1200s. Depending on which story you follow, he was travelling in France either on horseback or in a carriage when he was hard at his task. This would account for a few aberrations! Here and there we find a passage that spills over into the next chapter. That is why it is important to read on for a verse or two beyond the chapter end to avoid missing the connection. On the whole though, Stephen Langton did a good job, and the chapter and verse divisions make it much easier for us to locate a particular passage of Scripture.

Background

Having selected your book, if it is a New Testament epistle, it would be necessary to read the background details of the origins of the assembly to which the letter was sent. Thus the central portion of the Acts of the Apostles provides information about how the work of God was established in Galatia, Philippi, Thessalonica, Corinth and Ephesus. Familiarise yourself with the relevant historical account, and it might surprise you to find distinct link-ups between the story there, and things that are alluded to in the letter to that assembly.

Chapter 1

Now you are ready to proceed into the first chapter. You will have already noticed the leading themes of the book and noted these in what you may have called "The Introduction to the Book". Again, read and re-read the chapter carefully, and look out for where there is a transition of thought, so that what we call the divisions of the chapter become clear to you. You might decide that verses 1-5 form the first division; record that, and give the section a caption that will help you to remember the content of the verses. Do the same with the next section and so on.

Some Bible students have a flair for making all their summaries begin with the same letter of the alphabet and they find that method helps them to remember. I discovered early on that I did not possess that talent. It was very frustrating to find words beginning with the same letter for a couple of points then unable to think of any others! I made up my mind that the time being wasted in struggling to get a matching word was not worth the effort. You will have to discover for yourself whether you have that aptitude or not. One thing to avoid is using an obscure word or a word that is forced into service just for the sake of maintaining alliteration. Incidentally according to the definition of that figure of speech, real alliteration is when "a number of words, having the same consonant sound, occur close together in a series". For example, "round the rugged rock, the ragged rascal ran", or, "a big bully beats a baby boy". (Pardon the lesson in English grammar!).

Verse 1
Having divided the chapter and given suitable descriptions to each section, you now approach verse 1. With v.1 written in your margin, you are ready to record all your findings about the verse against that v.1! After reading it and thinking about it, you arrive at a decision about what it means, and the truth

being conveyed in its phrases. It might be a good idea to write out in your own words the meaning of the verse. (Normally first verses are fairly straightforward but I am using this as an example of how to approach every verse). At this stage, you may wish to read the verse in another translation. You can then turn your attention to its words, and this is where concordance work comes into play. You can discover and note the different shades of meaning of each word; you can see how the word is translated and used elsewhere in Scripture. Remember what I said earlier though; never allow your study of the individual words to obscure the thrust of what is being said in the sentence as a whole.

A fundamental rule of Bible study is that every statement must be interpreted in the light of the context in which it is found – what goes before it, what comes after it. If you lift statements out of their context, and place them side by side with statements that you have lifted out of other passages, you can get the Bible to say almost anything that you want it to say. It is a cliché but it bears another repeat! A text taken from its context becomes a pretext, and a pretext "is an excuse to say something that is not accurate". Context, context, context are the three fundamental rules of biblical interpretation! The Bible says, "There is no God" (Ps 14.1). It says, "there be gods many" (1 Cor 8 .5). It says, "there is one God" (1 Tim 2.5). Without taking context into account, these three statements are contradictory and two of them are misleading. So, the verses surrounding any given statement must be examined if a true understanding of the statement is to be achieved.

When considering your verse, another interesting line of approach is to ask yourself this question. "Is there any Old Testament story that illustrates this truth, or perhaps something in the Gospels or the Acts of the Apostles?" Illustrations from the world around us can be helpful, but there is nothing to match an example from the Bible itself. To be able to think about such illustrations, you would need to be constantly reading and becoming familiar with the historical books of the Bible. Some of these books may not lend themselves to the kind of in-depth Bible study that you would apply to a New Testament epistle, but to constantly read them will provide you with rich resources of biblical illustrations. They were "written for our learning" (Rom 15.4).

It has to be admitted, that there are some verses that are a more difficult to understand than others. Sometimes the thoughts and opinions of others who have been studying for a lot longer and have listened to much more Bible teaching can be helpful. Many have recorded their thoughts in what are generally known as **Bible Commentaries**. Do not go the commentary first when approaching a passage for study. Think about the verses for yourself, seek the guidance of the Holy Spirit, and then you may refer to some of these books to check if the author's thoughts coincide with yours, and to get that little bit of help from them as far as difficult passages are concerned.

It would be good to get some guidance on commentaries before splashing out a lot of money on an extensive "library". Books are not cheap; even second-hand dealers know the value of what they have available! Then, as to content, there are some publishing houses that have a distinct agenda as to the theology they are promoting. Some of it is well removed from what is generally believed by the assembly of Christians with whom you associate. It may be that a more mature believer could direct you to publications that may be helpful to you and pitched at a level that would suit your present needs. Some commentaries are very technical, and couched in such scholarly language as to be unintelligible to the average reader! Remember too that the commentary is not inspired, and you have to be discerning. Sometimes books that are 98% helpful have just that little bit in them that is off-beam, perhaps influenced by the spiritual environment of the author. You will probably find that some Bible apps that you have also include commentaries.

You continue to move from verse to verse then, exhilarated at times by your discoveries as you dig deeper, but at other times left with a feeling of being bogged down as you arrive at a difficulty that takes time to untangle. Keep pressing on though, and refuse to allow the complexity to turn your mind to something less demanding like catching up with the news or checking the other kind of texts that dominate our lives! When mental exertion is demanded, it is so easy to become distracted.

Chapter 8

CHARACTER STUDIES, THEMES AND TYPES

Bible Characters

Studying your verses, say in the epistles, you may come across a name that you recognise from a previous study, and it appeals to you to collect all the information that you can about that individual. For example, you will discover that Tychicus gets a first mention as one of Paul's travelling companions in the book of Acts, and then Paul refers to him when writing to the Ephesians, the Colossians, Timothy and Titus. You would read all these references to him and write down what is said about him in each. What kind of man was he, and what kind of things did he do? You will be asking, "Are there features in him that I should be copying? Are there mistakes that he made that I should be avoiding?" Exploring the background and behaviour of these individuals provides many practical lessons that will be helpful in Christian living. Again, your concordance will aid you to locate every reference to them. Just remember that some names have alternative spellings, e.g., Timothy and Timotheus.

We may not have many details of a man like Tychicus, but the biographies of characters such as Moses and Elijah occupy large areas of the Old Testament, with further references in the New Testament. It would be a major undertaking to investigate all the details of their lives, but think how worthwhile it would be! As with your studies of the epistles, try to be methodical, and divide your study into sections as you look at the different phases of their lives. Again, headings will be helpful as you record the details of their exploits and try to fix them firmly in your mind. Remember though, the purpose of your investigations is to learn practical lessons from their experiences that you can apply to yourself.

Themes

Another profitable way to study is to follow through a particular theme or doctrine. For example, if you were to read about redemption in Ephesians 1, it could spring to your mind that Peter also mentions it and you wonder about where else there are allusions to it. You would use your concordance or word check facility to discover the different references to the word. It would be good to write out the relevant verses and examine each. You will find that there are different aspects of redemption and you can explore these. You will see that there are different descriptions of the cost of redemption too, and a study of those would be good for your soul.

There are some subjects for which the concordance will not be of benefit. For example, should you see the undoubted value of exploring the subject of the deity of Christ, you will have no help as far as the word "deity" is concerned because it does not appear in Scripture. You will be dependent on your memory of passages with which you are familiar to start off your study. References in the margin of your Bible will lead you to other relevant passages, and they in turn to yet more. So gradually you build up your dossier of material with statements of His deity, evidences of His deity, and acknowledgements of His deity and so on.

Types

You may have heard of "typical teaching", and by that is meant the examination and explanation of Old Testament items, individuals or incidents that foreshadow either the Lord Jesus or Christian experience. For example, 1 Corinthians 10 contains a resume of Israel's history and declares that "all these things happened unto them for ensamples: and they are written for our admonition" (v.11). In other words, what happened to them contains serious lessons for believers of this Christian era. In light of that, many Bible students have found great profit in following the path of Israel with its twists and turns, its pitfalls and progress. They can see in the story of the vanquished slaves in Egypt becoming victorious soldiers in Canaan parallels with our own history as believers. A study like this, sometimes entitled, "From Egypt to Canaan", would keep you busy for a long time and would be a very worthwhile study to pursue.

In Romans 5.14, Adam is said to be "a figure (type) of him that was to come". This gives us authorisation for seeing in some Old Testament characters pictures, albeit imperfect pictures, of the Lord Jesus Christ. What is said about the meaning of Melchizedec's name and the meaning of Salem, the place where he reigned, show it is legitimate to make a point even from the meaning of Bible names and place names (Heb 7.2).

One of my first studies as a young person was to look at the life of Joseph and see in it features of the Saviour. It was encouraging to discover for myself what older believers had known for many years, that there are so many things about him and his experiences that prefigure the Lord Jesus. William MacDonald entitled his book on the life of Joseph, "Joseph reminds me of Jesus". As already noted, character studies can be gripping, but in some cases there is the added bonus of seeing Christ reflected in the individual being considered.

A reading of the Epistle to the Hebrews leaves us with the conviction that the tabernacle with its offerings and its priesthood and its Day of Atonement ritual was all pointing forward to something grander, as in the statement, "the law having a shadow of good things to come" (Heb 10.1). The foreshadowings were all imperfect, but there is so much about them that reveal heart-warming glimpses of our Saviour and the value of His work at the cross. To properly understand the Epistle to the Hebrews you would need at least some knowledge of these Old Testament sacrifices and rituals. This could be a more challenging consideration but there would be great profit in it.

It has to be said that some people have become disillusioned with typical teaching, and possibly the reason for that is that some Bible teaching has involved great flights of fancy and attempts to conjure up invalid applications. I have tried to provide brief scriptural allusions as to the validity of typical teaching, but I would caution against being fanciful. It is absolutely vital to have a biblical basis for making the link between aspects of a type and the Lord Jesus.

We must also have scriptural authority for identifying types, allowing us to make the leap from the shadow to the substance. We have talked about the experience of Israel in the wilderness and the lessons we can learn from them. There are also a number of things in the book of Exodus which point forward to the Saviour and we have New Testament sanction for making the link - the Passover lamb, the manna, and the smitten rock. These are just samples of many Old Testament items, which if explored, will unearth precious truth about our Saviour.

Chapter 9

THEORY OR PRACTICE?

It is to be hoped that a reading of the foregoing chapters will have given a few simple guidelines about how to go about the study of the most amazing book ever written. It may be that you are just a little more enlightened about the theory of how to study the Bible! The big issue now is, when will the theory be put into practice? Some of you may feel that when the pressure of the exams is over will be the time to get busy on it, or after some assignment is complete. Others may have looked at the suggestions about tools and helps and have come to the conclusion that when you surround yourself with all the recommended "equipment", that's the time to start being earnest. Listen, even the world knows the importance of striking when the iron is hot! The time for action is NOW! If reading this little booklet has fired you with enthusiasm for Bible study, get started on your adventure to explore the Book.

Just a final word of caution; the word "study" has been employed constantly throughout this little volume. The word itself is normally associated with "brain work", so there is the danger that we could approach the Scriptures in a purely academic fashion, cramming our heads with knowledge and failing to allow what we learn to impact our lives. The study of Scripture must be approached prayerfully, with a conscious dependence on the Holy Spirit, for God reveals things to us "by his Spirit" (1 Cor 2.10).

A submissive attitude is necessary, and the determination to work out our discoveries in daily living. "Ezra had prepared his heart to seek the law of the Lord, **and to do it**, and to teach in Israel statutes and judgments" (Ezra 7.10). Notice the order; preparation of heart, leading to application to the Word, leading to living its teaching, leading to communicating its truth to others. That order should never be disturbed. The person who has never allowed the Word to mould his own behaviour is in no position to impose its teaching on others. That is the kind of hypocrisy that marked the Pharisees and brought about severe criticism from the Saviour; "they say, and do not" (Mt 23.3). There is nothing worse than to encounter someone who appears to be brim-full of Bible knowledge and yet their attitude to others is superior and critical, unkind and uncaring. Genuine, prayerful Bible study should produce Christlikeness.

Another danger in accumulating a knowledge of the Scriptures is the desire to parade that knowledge! Young men, don't be tempted to display your Bible knowledge in the prayer meeting. It is true that in the Bible, prayers were frequently laced with relevant quotations from Scripture, but never use the prayer meeting to exhibit what you have learned; you are there to pray sincerely and earnestly about specific needs and to give thanks to God.

A weekly Bible Study can be another area of danger. In your personal studies while preparing for the meeting, you will have forged convictions about the meaning of each verse that is being considered. It might just be that someone else will express an alternative view on some point. If they are obviously in error it would have to be challenged, but never debate any issue in a quarrelsome way. Voices should never be raised, courtesy should always be maintained and respect should always be displayed. The purpose of the Bible Study is the promotion not only of an understanding of the Word, but also of the spiritual wellbeing of those present.

In conclusion then, *read* the Word, *meditate* on the Word, *study* the Word, but above all, all *receive* "the engrafted word" with meekness, and *do* it. James says, "*be ye doers* of the word" for therein lies the blessing; "this man shall be blessed in his deed" (Jas 1.21-25).